MINIMALISM

The Ultimate Guide to the Minimalist Lifestyle

(Tips and Ideas on How to Live a Stress-free Life With Minimalism)

Lottie Walker

Published By Jordan Levy

Lottie Walker

All Rights Reserved

Minimalism: The Ultimate Guide to the Minimalist Lifestyle (Tips and Ideas on How to Live a Stress-free Life With Minimalism)

ISBN 978-1-77485-285-9

All rights reserved. No part of this guide may be reproduced in any form without permission in writing from the publisher except in the case of brief quotations embodied in critical articles or reviews.

Legal & Disclaimer

The information contained in this book is not designed to replace or take the place of any form of medicine or professional medical advice. The information in this book has been provided for educational and entertainment purposes only.

The information contained in this book has been compiled from sources deemed reliable, and it is accurate to the best of the Author's knowledge; however, the Author cannot guarantee its accuracy and validity and cannot be held liable for any errors or omissions. Changes are periodically made to this book. You must consult your doctor or get professional medical advice before using any of the suggested remedies, techniques, or information in this book.

Upon using the information contained in this book, you agree to hold harmless the Author from and against any damages, costs, and expenses, including any legal fees potentially resulting from the application of any of the information provided by this guide. This disclaimer applies to any damages or injury caused by the use and application, whether directly or indirectly, of any advice or information presented, whether for breach of contract, tort, negligence, personal injury, criminal intent, or under any other cause of action.

You agree to accept all risks of using the information presented inside this book. You need to consult a professional medical practitioner in order to ensure you are both able and healthy enough to participate in this program.

TABLE OF CONTENTS

INTRODUCTION 1

CHAPTER 1: THE FIRST CHAPTER IS ABOUT MINIMALISM .. 7

CHAPTER 2: PRINCIPLES OF MINIMALISM 21

CHAPTER 3: DON'T GIVE. 37

CHAPTER 4: CHAOS STRESS, AND UNPRODUCTIVENESS .. 45

CHAPTER 5: MINIMALISM VS. FAST-FASHION VS. CONSCIOUS SHOPPING 52

CHAPTER 6: THE WAY TO SKYROCKET COMMUNICATION SKILLS 62

CHAPTER 7: WHAT TO START 73

CHAPTER 8: MINIMALISM AT WORK 82

CHAPTER 9: DE-CLUTTERING THE MIND 89

CHAPTER 10: DEVISE A NEW SYSTEM OR ORGANIZATION 96

CHAPTER 11: ELIMINATING OF CLUTTER, EXCESS STUFF, AND SENTIMENTAL ITEMS... 103

CHAPTER 12: PREPARING FOR THE CHANGE................. 116

CHAPTER 13: LEARN ABOUT THE MINIMALIST LIFESTYLE 122

CHAPTER 14: THE MINIMALIST MAKEOVER - GETTING STARTED... 131

CHAPTER 15: BENEFITS OF MINIMALISTIC LIVING 155

CHAPTER 16: DE-CLUTTERING AND ORGANISING YOUR PERSONAL ITEMS 167

CONCLUSION 177

Introduction

It's nice to have less. This is the reason it's time to let go of everything else to go to the end of the road. This introduction is a simplified version of the message contained in this book that I'd like to communicate. I would like to show you the pleasure it is having less knowing that this is the total opposite of what makes you content, which is not the way we were taught. We believe we'll be happier with the less we have. The future isn't certain which is why we're saving and conserving as much as we can.

"Bigger can be better." This phrase is used by millions of individuals. In the majority of countries and cultures it is believed that having more and doing more things leads to happiness and a sense of value has been knit. Materialism, I'd claim, is an epidemic that is spreading far beyond our control. There is a widespread depressing feeling that the most frequent expression I encounter when I talk to people is "I would love to have an automobile" or "my life would be so much simpler when I had the money to buy it. "It implies that we require plenty of money and then we gradually begin to judge people on the amount of money they have. We start to see that money can solve a lot of our issues. If you pay the right price it is possible to change individuals' minds. If you are able to buy the minds of others, then you certainly can purchase happiness. Sure, you'll have to earn a lot of money, and you're definitely not missing any growth. You'll need everybody else to invest their money in you to earn money and that's the way it works.

Minimalism is the art of which you limit your possessions to a minimum amount that are of use. Living in a minimalist environment with only the essentials only brought benefits superficial for example, the enjoyment of having a neat home as well as the convenience of cleaning, but it has also resulted in a deeper change. This has given me the opportunity to consider what it means to be content. I've said goodbye to many things, including some I've been able to enjoy for a long time. Yet, each day, I have a an optimistic heart. Being minimalist has makes me feel more content than I did earlier.

I was always comparing myself with others, even though I had better or better things. This often caused me to be unsatisfied. I wasn't sure how to improve things. I couldn't concentrate on anything and have always wasted my time. In focusing all of our attention on what we have and what we would like to have and do not pay attention to other important aspects like our relationships, well-being and even our health. I can recall the time where my self-esteem was mostly based on what I had. I'd also belittle people who didn't have as much of possessions as I did. In the end, I was at a place where people were concerned most about the things I had, and not what kind of person I was. It is a pity to see people especially loved ones struggling to maintain a smile only because they lack the things they require or, in some instances, kill themselves every day due to having been overwhelmed with things to accomplish. They are unfairly denied their contentment, their time and hard-earned money. I'd like others to understand that less is more and actually enjoyable. I must educate people on how to be the kings of the world with what they already have. Living a minimalist lifestyle doesn't mean you have to sacrifice your comfort or sacrificing luxurious lifestyle.

In the same way, a revolution is happening which is expected to change the way we think about our environment and what is around us. The new and revolutionary revolution is the one of minimalistism. The process of organizing and cleaning your house can be a fantastic task because of clutter. This is particularly the case if you're not doing your best to practice minimalist living. This book aims to aid you in cleaning your house and teach you to use minimal agency in the process. This book offers a variety of tips strategies, methods, and techniques that can help you organize your home and maintain it in a clean orderly and quickly throughout the year. You could be cleaning every room in your home and providing you with tried-and-true minimal methods of organizing. These methods are organized into an easy layout that is easy to follow with useful instructions along the process. Let's start now and find out how to be the minimalist you are.

Chapter 1: The First Chapter Is About Minimalism.

Minimalism is an idea that has gained a lot of attention quickly. Like many concepts that gain rapid acceptance, misconceptions about the notion are frequent.

Certain people believe that minimalism is to be the monks' way of life. Others believe it's about living an uncomfortable lifestyle of an ascetic. Many people are concerned that their lives could be very difficult if they decide to go minimalist. Others are of the opinion that minimalistism will cause them to be isolated from society.

If you've also had these thoughts This book will assist you in understanding the idea of minimalism more fully. This book will serve as your guide to understanding the ins and outs of minimalism.

Minimalism isn't something just for the wealthy. It's also not a way to create a style statement. It's easy to understand and isn't cost-effective even. It's simply living a lifestyle which gives you greater freedom and more space.

The most effective way to define minimalistism is to say it's a way to live a simpler but satisfying life. The idea must be absorbed for a bit.

The modern world is that a an easy and enjoyable life could appear strange in a single sentence. If you're also thinking this way, it's not your own. We've been taught the belief that "the more the better'. But, it is crucial to look into the reasoning behind that claim.

Just a century ago the world was quite different. It was a place of limitations and anxieties. Only those with the most riches could believe they were entitled. Others lived in poverty and in utter poverty. This increased the need to acquire ever more.

Food security, extravagant lifestyle, and the abundance are new concepts. The world has gone through many changes and our previous generations have witnessed a brutal history. It's left an impression in us that possessions of material wealth can bring our security and bring happiness.

This impression does nothing to benefit us. We've made ourselves the slaves of objects. We've worked hard to acquire these things without considering their value for our own lives. We haven't given an thought to whether the items we have accumulated to make us feel content are actually bringing us satisfaction or not.

The quest to acquire ever more is making us a shopper. We are simply trying to accumulate all we can. It's not a surprise that Americans have an overall part of 4.29 percent, experienced an astonishing retail spending of $5.7 trillion in 2017. This was during an era when worldwide retail spending was $22.64 trillion. It is a sign that people in the US all by themselves, with just a 5% share of the world, purchased 25% of all goods produced around the world.

It's gone way beyond the need to buy things and security. Consumption has become a routine. That's where all the problems start.

The desire for ever more things has taken away the rationale for purchasing the product. Nowadays, people shop not to purchase things, but because they are feeling like shopping. It's become a popular activity to do.

The act of buying things has become an opportunity to express yourself. It's become a trend in such a way that there are many kinds of consumers.

There's a category called "Compulsive Shopaholics". They shop to relieve anxiety. The purchase of things that might not be needed is now a method to relieve anxiety.

There's a different category of shoppers referred to as "Trophy Shopaholics'. They shop until they find the ideal variation. What they'd do with their previous purchases is anybody's speculation.

There is also the category of "Flashy Spenders". They go shopping in order to turn into the biggest spenders. They buy items to prove themselves to be the people with deep pockets, and will end up emptying their pockets.

There's a different category of buyers known as "Collectors'. They want everything. Every color, variation designs, brands You name it, and they'd like to own it. They are aware that they may not utilize all the items they're purchasing. However, they're making purchases because they have an the insatiable desire of having all of it. They are insatiable with the desire of the Emperors.

Shopping isn't an issue that is restricted to the rich and powerful only. Even those with small pockets enjoy shopping at the malls. They are the most ardent target of the retail chains since they have deep desire to purchase the best they can, and are willing to go to extreme lengths to achieve this. They'll ask for money and then take out loans. Credit at astronomical interest rates. Enjoy life with EMIs. Cyber Monday Black Friday, Labor Day, Memorial Day president's day and independence day sale New Year's Day sale, all of them are designed to draw this particular segment. They are known as 'Bargain shoppers'. They'd purchase things that they do not want with the money they do not have, just because the seller claims that it's inexpensive. The items purchased may not be used and remain in the trash and create chaos.

There's another type of consumers called "Bulimic Shoppers". They are not satisfied with what they purchase. They continue to go around and around trying to find a better product. The frequent trips make consumers buy more, which is costlier and more expensive. The shoppers continue to tell themselves that they're getting the best exchange. In the process they also purchase the new models, as well as making the old ones more expensive to levels they could not pay for in the first place.

The final result of these habits of spending is a house packed with items they do not want. However, since they've purchased them, they are able to throw them away. They are forced to pay for items they don't need. They are left with items you do not want. They are living an extravagant lifestyle and yet, a life of compromises. It's a sad life. In the name of living the American Dream They are living an uneasy life which is why they are caught in a cycle of debt and unhappiness. They are never content. They constantly want more, not thinking about how they will use their items. Then comes the difficult task of keeping these things. It is a laborious process and cash to maintain them. There are more things to clean and repairs. This can mean more stress and cost. People always feel constrained.

Spending more means that you have more debt to pay. This is a vicious circle that is very difficult to break. The majority of people are caught in the cycle of spending and earning. The time to enjoy the things you have never arrives. People are willing to sacrifice their family time, happiness and love for the ability to spend more money. They technically are free, however, for practical purposes they are trapped by their own heads. They are slaves to their habit of acquiring many new things to acquire.

Through this entire procedure, the reason to own possessions is defeated. You purchase things to ensure that you can use them. That 72" Flat Screen UHD TV that you purchased at the cost of hours of your time won't be of any value if you don't actually have time to spend watching it. It's just a piece of equipment to display. The pleasure fades when the person you were hoping to impress gets a new version of the television. There is more than one person that is racing. It's a gruelling race that has no end. It's a way towards the end of satisfaction.

This attitude is not just impacting you as an individual but is also taking a the toll upon your loved ones. The time you spend with your family keeps getting reduced. The members of your family keep learning the useless art of having possessions. This is affecting the fabric of the family unit.

Minimalism can help you escape the trap of having increasing amounts of stuff and moving towards the notion of "Less is More' so that you can take advantage of what you can afford to enjoy. It's an empowering concept which helps you live an enjoyable life. It allows you to get your family members on the same page and live an enjoyable and peaceful life.

Minimalism doesn't mean being less, it's about having only those items you need, not things that you would like to have. It helps you understand that your needs are not unlimited, but desires are endless. If you decide to live a life of wanting then you will be sacrificing your life for your endless desires , and never feeling satisfied.

Alexander the great world conqueror his empire span to 2 million miles, and three continents. He was awash with all the way to offer from Greece up to Danube as well as Egypt to India however, when he passed away, he would like that his tomb was laid with his hands wide open, so that all the world could observe that even the most powerful conqueror in the world could not require more than 6 square feet of space.

Minimalism can assist you in getting from the habit of having a plethora of things to possess the things you require and take pleasure in. This is a method that will allow families to stay together as a group and enjoy being together.

This book can assist you to understand what minimalism is as well as how you can integrate it in your family. It will assist you live an active and meaningful life, where you are able to make informed choices about what you want. You'll be able to manage things in a much better way and will have more control over the desires of your have things.

This book will show ways you can create a minimalist house that does not require constant work. It will allow you to spend more time with your family and to pursuing your interests.

The LA Times report suggests that the average American family has more than 300,000 belongings. A Daily Mail report suggests that throughout our lives, we could be spending on average 3680 hours, or 150 days searching for lost things in our homes. It also discovered that we can lose up to 9 items per day on a basis or 193,743 during the course of our lives. The more items we own to lose, the more confused we become.

An Fox Business report says that on average , an American can spend up to $300,000. over the course of a lifetime to purchase items which aren't necessary. The Wall Street Journal states that annually American consumption of non-essential items is $1.2 trillion. This is a significant amount of money going to items that aren't needed in a time where people and families are in a state of struggle with debt and mortgages.

These habits aren't just making our lives more difficult, but they also make the homes we live in smaller. Our homes are being surrounded with clutter, which isn't helping anyone. A house that is overflowing with clutter requires more maintenance and cleaning and this, in turn, requires the time and money.

The book 'Minimalism for Families' can assist you understand the consequences of this habit of uncontrolled spending and accumulation of stuff. It will give you specific strategies for cleaning up items and have a home which is more organized and less stressful. You will be able to manage your finances more efficiently and allocate your money to areas that need more focus.

Chapter 2: Principles Of Minimalism

It's free.

The pursuit of the most minimal approach to life is not a cost to you nothing. If you are awestruck by photos of minimalist modern Scandinavian furniture it might be tempting to buy similar furniture for your own home, but this is the other side of minimalistism. Living a minimalist lifestyle does not mean you have to purchase items that are minimalist in design. The most effective method to start is by getting rid of the clutter around your home that are not bringing in money, and then persevering with implementing the items that you have.

The system is dynamic.

Minimalism isn't something that can be done in a single time. It might start out with a small amount of effort, but the effect on the environment, its benefits and the way it appears will develop as time passes. Although it may feel luxurious to get to a point of decluttering you feel at ease about, be aware that it can change with time. What you define as minimalism for you may change depending on your lifestyle and needs. alter.

First, clear the clutter, then prepare for the for the second

Instead of spending time organizing, you can keep in the garage, and strengthen yourself and organization to work by clearing out the things first. The first step is to declutter and then organize the rest. It's easier to organize when you've got less stuff.

Avoid letting the desire for factors interfere with your work

One of the main guiding principles of minimalism is to not let matters or need to achieve things stand out of your way of doing the thing that truly is important to you. What that means is letting go off anything you don't need and reducing the flow of news so that you can take it in slow and focus on the most important aspects.

There's not a plethora of devices

There's not a lot that you can try to get with minimal. Be concerned about whether you've got more than 100 things in your home is just as bad as buying more than you need. In both cases there is a risk of an over-emphasis on the things. Don't be worried about the huge range of options, but think of the concept of minimalism as a way to keep letting go of the things you're ready to get rid of.

There's no need to swap stories in exchange for things.

There are quite a few studies that suggest that the reports are superior to things. However, other studies have been published stating that the deliberate purchase of both items and experiences are what makes you the most happy. There's no need to swap one unintentional behaviour for another. It's about making conscious choices in general.

Separating your self-esteem from the possessions you have

One of the most surprising but crucial effect of minimalism is confidence I've gained in myself. As you purge and consume less, you'll realize that your self-confidence does not depend on the kind of clothes you wear, the model of car you drive, or what furniture you've acquired. The things that you own don't define who you are in any way, but rather help you to declutter your more valuable or sentimental items.

It's about building your decision muscles

Particularly if you're starting out to work with minimalism, you should start by working in a smaller scale at the first day. Start with the simple items first, and then store the larger items to use later. Utilize the method of decluttering to build your muscle of choice. As you make more and more decisions about what you want and don't need for your life, you'll be better at making conscious choices. The development of this muscle allows you to live a more intentional life as time passes.

There's no need to worry about an easier time living

Minimalism isn't about living in a simpler life. It might be easy however it's not easy. The motivation behind of minimalism is the need to create an extra space to work on more with what you are interested in you are interested in, learning about the various aspects and facing larger problems. The concept of minimalism is getting rid of distractions so you can make more significant contribution.

The ability to reduce your size helps you get things done

We all know what it's like to like to be juggling many tasks that you don't even know how to begin. Minimalism doesn't just refer to the things. It could be the chores such as to-do lists, lists of tasks and obligations we assume. It helps you delegate tasks that aren't essential to allow you to devote more concentration and time to complete the ones you really need. In removing the piles of work You're removing the distractions that keep you from getting anything done even a bit.

Determine The Most Important

The following simple way to simplify your life is to determine the things that are most essential to your daily life. If you aren't aware of what is essential to you, there's no way to set priorities for your daily life. Greg Mckeown in his ebook Essentialism describes the role of a story in another's life in the absence of defining what's important and what's not. We get used to doing what we're taught we have to do. The key is to follow the principles of minimalism and creating a clear area for attention to be focused to what topics are most important. Thus, you should determine the most important things for you, and not what you're told to desire. If you are aware of your needs, it's easy to decide what is compatible with your lifestyle and what's not.

The most effective way to start to set your priorities is to review of your calendar. Are there any items that could be eliminated to make your life more simple?

Reduce your time commitments by refusing to accept requests you don't need. It doesn't mean you're trying to be completely unsocial. It does recommend saying "no" more often, so that you are able to be able to say "yes" to things that matter on you.

Simple standards are a way to simplify your life is about establishing and respecting your limits.

Clear Your Closet

Even if you don't get rid of everything in your house, removing your closets will take you by in the direction of simplifying your life. The problem of decision fatigue is real. With a reduction in the variety of gadgets for clothing or the assistance of creating a tablet-based wardrobe, you will reduce the number of choices you must make each morning. It's no longer necessary to stare into your closet and think that I don't have anything I want to wear. If you alter your attitude regarding your clothes your life will reflect that change. Remove the clothes you don't enjoy and never wear. You should feel beautiful in everything that you wear. First, get all of the clothes out of the closet first. Make three piles: one to collect donations, one for items to get rid of, and the third one is for gadgets you'll use. Put the things you'll need to put back in the closet. Then, follow the steps and donate or dispose of the other gadgets.

Stop buying things you don't Really Need

I'm not going to lie Retail therapy can be beneficial, but only to get a quick and easy moment. It usually leads to more stress and guilt throughout our life. The analysis of your motivations in the background of spending money is a basic principle that can help you to make the most of your money. It won't help in reducing your spending but it will make sure that when you do spend money, it's for things that you truly desire or love.

If you've been working long and hard to clean your property, and the last thing you'll would like to do is clutter it all over again with objects you don't need. Instead, you should take the time to think about your purchases

Practice Mono-tasking

It's commonplace to do multiple things at the same time. The way we live our lives is based on the idea that multi-tasking is hook or by the crook a virtue. The reality is that multi-tasking is in violation of almost all, if there is any, but not every, of the minimalist notions. To make your life easier and not be distracted it is crucial to pay attention to your current tasks as well as the things you're getting rid of. Research shows that mono-tasking, and not multitasking is the rule of the game for get things done. The reason is that the brain wasn't necessarily designed to focus on several tasks at once. We switch between tasks in a flash. Therefore, instead of multitasking, focus of the ability to focus on one task at a time. Reduce the amount of work that you're working on, you'll be able to accomplish more in less time.

Make Rhythms and Routines

I'm a huge advocate of having routines and rhythms built into your daily routine because they will help you put things in autopilot. A well-planned evening routine can allow you to start the next day with a positive attitude. It stops the morning of chaos since you're prepared for everything that needs to be completed ahead of the time. You can carry on your routine throughout the day by way of having a tough and quick sequence of tasks to complete which will allow you to begin your day more at ease. I've also discovered that a simple routine for cleansing can make it easier to manage all household chores. The rhythms and exercises will are a great way to eliminate unnecessary while at the same time as automating the tasks that must be completed. Make an evening routine, a morning routine or just about anything! Setting up a routine that is clean and consistent will make life easier because they provide the steps-by-step method to accomplish your goals to give more attention to the things that matter most.

Plan Your Week

If you're looking to simplify but don't know how to begin your everyday scheduling classes is the ideal place to start. This is the place that I'm accustomed to doing and I am sure that organizing your life will make it much simpler. One good way to start is to note down your top priorities for the coming week. This will enable you to see the specifics of what you want to see completed. The next step is to review the activities for the week, and make sure you have time for the important things. Additionally, create a fashionable food plan that is primarily based upon your schedule to plan your week. Even if my day doesn't follow exactly the plan the fact that I have a plan to start will make it easier to handle any unexpected things that could arise.

Eat well

There is no better location to explore the simple principles of getting rid of excess waste that when it comes to eating properly. The majority of the packaged food that is found in grocery stores are stuffed full of processed junk. This isn't essential and most of it could be harmful to your health. This isn't declaring that you must in no way indulge in junk food or treats food items. Truthfully I have massive sweet tooth and never refuse to eat any chocolate item. But, it is best to indulge in moderate amounts. Remember that your top diet should consist exclusively of whole, fresh food items. The reality is that there is things that make life more quickly than being unwell. Consume what you like with moderate amounts, however be aware about what foods keep you well. Make sure you do some form of regular exercise and observe how much easier living is by cutting out unnecessary food items in your diet.

Make Every Thing count

Whatever you decide to accomplish, try to make it worth your while. The reason why my most memorable day by a realization that we often go through the motions of doing what's expected of us instead of taking in the moment that we're in. This means that we overlook those important moments that we never will ever get another chance at. If we're not actively in making life simpler, complex prevails every time. The practice of living with simple principles is about purpose in all activities we undertake. Connect with those who are part of your lives. Spend time with your friends in the interest of being social. Meet for coffee instead of texting or, at a minimum, pick up the phone and make a call. Enjoy meaningful conversations with your fellow humans. Discover new things and new spots. While you're there you should take plenty of photographs. When you've finished the day, think about your actions and reflect on the things you could do better.

Chapter 3: Don't Give.

We've all heard, "It is better to give rather than accept." While it may sound like a cliché, the truth is that giving, in any form, is a certain crucial factor to achievement.

It's possible that you don't have the time, the energy or funds to contribute especially during the most stressful and challenging moment in your life. Be aware, however there is a good chance that everybody has something worth giving and by giving, you'll receive satisfaction, good vibes and feelings back.

If you offer either your money, time, or skills, you'll receive abundance of gratitude and joy as a result. When a happy recipient greets you with a smile or shakes your hand and praises your work on their behalf, the happiness and warmth are likely to overflow your body as they wash away your worries and sorrow as pure and pure joy flow inward. In a flash, you'll be able to feel appreciated, loved and more confident. your faith in humanity will be renewed because you have made a significant positive impact on the world.

When you learn to appreciate and really savor the smallest gestures (the handshakes and words of praise or the words of praise, etc.) In doing this, you're becoming aware of the beauty of minimalist living. You can take time to appreciate and get great satisfaction from the smallest things which really can be so meaningful.

Take a look. If you get a pay check for a job well-done then you'll earn money you need to pay your bills this week, or as we would believe! However, when someone says that your "job well-done could have changed the course of your life or saved a life, these are those that boost your spirits and ensure your existence.

Additionally, you will gain from the experience of giving in particular if you donate in a manner that makes the most of your skills and interests. You will be able to have fun and have fun using your talents and gifts to help others. Your self-confidence and self-esteem will increase and so will your overall sense of contentment and joy. It is possible that you will discover an entirely new purpose for your life and gain (please forget the cliché) the possibility of a fresh start on your life!

Researchers have also discovered that those who volunteer are happier and are more likely to live longer, with less depression, higher satisfaction with their lives and improved overall well-being (source). So what are you sitting around to do? Give it a shot!

Apart from financial donations that any organisation will take note of, you can bring almost any talent or interest to the art of giving back. Here are a few examples:

How to Give

Do you have a good understanding of construction or building? You can build your own home in the name of Habitat for Humanity; an international nonprofit that provides low-cost, low-interest housing to families in need. Volunteer to construct an animal kennel in an animal shelter in the area.

Are you a great listener and speaking? Consider becoming the crisis counselor in an area mental health clinic. The more you are focused on the issues of others, the less your own personal issues will take over your thoughts.

Are you a gifted musician? Do you want to volunteer to sing or play music in an area nursing home where residents are certain to be enthused by classic tunes that bring them back of their childhood.

You are a great storyteller or wordsmith? Create and perform your stories to children in need in youth centers, or at your local Boys and Girls Club.

Do you have a knack for sewing or quilting? Create some clothing to give to the local shelter for domestic violence or to The Salvation Army.

Do you love sports? Run a team of athletes for children who would not have had the thrill of hitting a goal or a home run. They when they play keep themselves out of trouble and developing new techniques.

Are you a pro when it comes to cooking? Prepare meals in an in-home soup kitchen or instruct people with limited income to prepare healthy and affordable meals.

Are you a person with a talent to the drama? Create a theater group in your community for children who are struggling financially; give them the chance to shine and a artistic relief from their stress-filled lives.

There is a good chance that many charities in your region are seeking volunteers of all types and if you spot an untapped or unserved population in your neighborhood create your own club or long-term effort which can meet this need.

Personally I've also composed news articles and press releases in order to raise funds for non-profit organisations of all types and types, from children's charity to shelters for domestic violence. I've also hosted charity book-signings on behalf of worthy organizations like Toys for Tots and Sunrise sexual and domestic violence center. I have experienced immense joy and satisfaction from giving, just as I could from presenting millions of dollars to of these amazing organisations. It's all about the small things.

In short, the more time and energy you invest in helping other people, the less time that you'll be able to suffer from suffering; that constant whirlpool of stress, anxiety and stress that is often threatening to take over your life. There are new people who you can talk to and connect with. Some of them could be able to provide helpful advice that can help you solve some of the issues that you face. At the very most, you will be able to be able to share the joy of being generous.

Your heart will be filled and your spirit elevated, and you may discover that you love serving others.

Chapter 4: Chaos Stress, And Unproductiveness

One of the most effective methods to reduce your efficiency at work or at home is to be surrounded by clutter. A messy space can negatively impact your mood, energy levels and capability to work efficiently not even forgetting the stress that it causes.

Additionally, a cluttered house can create stress and anxiety for the mind and body, mostly due to the fact that living in such an area may make you feel that you don't have control over your living space, and consequently living a life.

The problem is that a messy environment hinders the ability of you to focus, and also your brain's ability take in information. The reason is that clutter makes you feel distracted; it is a battle for your attention, and, as you've probably guessed that it isn't feasible to resist it each time, and this can increase your anger. Your mental capacity slowly wears away and quickly spiral into mental and emotional frustration. However hard you do, you will never be productive in a setting or in such a situation.

You're aware that you must take action but as the stress grows, the mess you're faced with seems to be overwhelming just to think about. If you do not confront the clutter, there's a chance that you'll add to the amount of mess. This leaves you feeling pressured and in a state of confusion, never knowing what to do first (addressing the mess, and perhaps which items to keep and which to eliminate) and this could result in serious psychological issues like anxiety.

Note: Being constantly stressed or every day alters the brain's physical structure which makes it more sensitive to stress.

Why? because it is a stress-related hormone called cortisol.

If you're always stressed, the stress hormone increases and travels to the amygdala brain region which is known as the 'alarm centre'. The stress hormone also kills neurons that make up the hippocampus. another brain area that, in addition, is responsible for visual memory and controlling emotions. The mental stress experience in particular, when it becomes persistent or extreme, can slowly alter the structure of the brain. This means it could result in you becoming more at risk of stress.

Where Did All the Chaos Come From, To Start With?

There are a myriad of reasons we accumulate clutter. It could be due to incessant buying urges, the memories from the past and emotions (that cause us to hold on to items we don't want) or the worry about having to get rid of something that we may require in the future, guilt or obligation and maybe even hoping for an improvement.

It is a natural for you to be an emotional person. That's why you tend to imbue your possessions with feelings. In various ways, you see the items as a an integral part of you or as a reflection of yourself. You can imagine it can make the process of clearing out your clutter extremely difficult.

Let's consider a basic example.

Someone I know keeps the same blanket from childhood. She's had numerous conversations with her partner regarding the blanket which is more than 20 years old but at the time of day, in addition to being tucked under other blankets, it's not getting any use. According to her, it's crucial for her that the blanket remains in exactly the same as it was when she even got angry in the past five years when her friend attempted to wash it.

The blanket is in fact an integral piece of her. It smells exactly like her; it looks and feels familiar and is constantly reminding her of the memories of her childhood. To her it is the only blanket that can ever be as warm or offer the similar warmth.

For some of us our possessions might not be the things you call 'cherished friends from old however, they convey a lot about us. Different kinds of clutter communicate various emotional signals.

If, for instance, your clutter is mostly items from others or other people, then you're probably one of the people who struggle with the boundaries. If your clutter is mostly memories (or souvenirs) of the past, then you aren't able to let things go or to feel that your most memorable times are now behind you.

If the clutter you have is mostly empty things, then you likely feel a phobia or a sense of uncertainty or a skepticism about the future. This could be an indication that you'd like to be something else. The thought of spending you time being a fashion-conscious icon could have sounded better than the actual act.

Then, there are projects that have not been completed. According to many psychologists who explain, this chaos is caused by perfectionists. It's always your belief that you could make it more perfect than it actually is; the problem is that it's not perfect enough and you won't ever complete it. The unfinished projects serve as constantly reminders of our incompetence on the things we've have set out to accomplish. It's a glare and can be a depressing experience.

Whatever the reason or the reason why your clutter is taking over any space in your home, you can remove it in easy steps. As the next paragraph will demonstrate that you don't need expensive tools to get rid of clutter or tidy your office and home.

Chapter 5: Minimalism Vs. Fast-Fashion Vs. Conscious Shopping

Certain items we normally think of as expensive are readily present in every shopping center we visit - increasing in massive stores. They are usually available in what we would call "fast shops for fashion" that you have heard of and likely have walked into. They are identified by having a variety of pieces on ready and in every size available, divided into different varieties.

The stores are renowned for their the value and accessibility of our clothes. Simply walk into the shop, select (several) latest and more affordable products, test them out and make your way to the cash register. It's so inexpensive to purchase new products ranging from clothing to shoes - that many consumers don't really think on the caliber of what they buy and they think about the possibility of fixing what we are already wearing in our closets instead of purchasing new items.

However, beyond our beloved minimalism, there are additional reasons to consider purchasing less and using less environmental impact.

The act of buying (and obviously throwing away) excessive clothing and accessories is not sustainable.

One example: the majority of garments are made from cotton. its production requires the use of a variety of pesticides and chemicals - in fact as per The Elephant Journal, the cotton production is responsible for anywhere from 11 percent to 12% of all pesticides utilized in the world.

Additionally to that, not only could the manufacturing of raw materials cause an environmental issue and the environment, but also the removal of these materials: Have ever wondered where those clothes, t-shirts, shoes or other things you no longer want go? You'll probably be able to reveal what the used items help those who need it However, they will also get a lot of donations. In the end they'll also have to dispose of.

The whole process could end up in the form of garbage and each year the volume of waste we create grows, and in the near future there will be no where to store our trash for a long time. In third world countries, it's quite common to find horrible examples of dumpsters in open air that can't be recycled.

Yet even if we were to focus on specific fast-fashion companies which have been implicated in serious scandals We have a further reason to be concerned about excessive consumption of clothing, whether by children or slave work.

Some businesses (not all obviously) operate factories in countries that employ less labor than in their home country. At present, all is fairly well - the problem has been that young children have been discovered working in these factories , as well as employees working longer hours than what the law would allow, or earning less than the minimum wage in their local area. This is considered slave labor.

All in order to satisfy the desire of human beings to get more than they actually need.

That's how we go back to the minimalist lifestyle. A limited closet, after all, has more than one function: to be more environmentally-friendly and humanly correct, lighten your pocket and make your life easier when it comes to dressing.

We were all that were born and raised in the economic system; consumption is part of our norm - films and TV shows have taught us the need purchase cool and new items constantly. The media taught us that "if you can't afford to buy the latest trends and you don't have the money to buy it, you're likely to be a loser" and "people at work can't observe me in identical clothes twice within the same month"

This isn't the case, particularly because I can promise that when you go to your college, work or family gatherings and wear the same outfit more than three or two times, no one will notice. Two things to consider making sure the clothing are neat and well-maintained. In addition it's all good as people will not notice or in the event that they do, they are likely to assume that these are your top style and won't be bothered to inquire why you wear that outfit numerous times.

Let's test it out:

Choose a shirt you like , and head to work on Monday. Repeat the same outfit on the following Friday. If this shirt isn't in extremely flashy colors or particular details, nobody will be able to tell or believe that it's a problem. If, of course you neglect to wash your clothes. And make sure you remember to do that.

Step-by-stepguide on how to design an uncluttered wardrobe

It could be confusing. However, I assure you that it's not. It's actually fun.

Here are some of my suggestions:

Accept the fact that you have way too many clothes.

Shop for your own clothing:

Get all your clothes out of your closetand then categorize everything clothes, pants coats, t-shirts, coats... whatever you'd like.

Begin to select your top items - like that top you love, the shirt that makes you smile and pants that feel so comfy that you'd wear them for every day.

Take a look at the other pieces of clothing and consider: "if I go shopping this morning and saw these clothes do I want to buy them?"

If you get the answer "maybe" when you feel nervous about putting these items aside, here's one idea: grab a large box and store everything you own that are a source of doubt and a note that includes the date you placed them away. Then, give an expiration date to the item: if you don't have a need for it for, say 6 months, that means you don't actually need it. However, you shouldn't place all your clothes in this category because If you do, you'll never be able to throw away things you don't want.

The clothes you really love and require after that are folded and store in your closet. Other pieces you don't need any more, should be thrown away.

You now have to learn to live only with those items that remain after the cleaning process. After you've gotten comfortable with your new wardrobe , can you allow yourself to shop for any other items you consider as necessary. Be sure to purchase only what you require and not that shirt that says "oh it's 50 percent off, and I'll need it someday because it's so inexpensive!"

Consider the things which will be taken out Sort things into bags or boxes and decide what you want to do with them. Most of the stuff in your closet ought to be in good condition (at at least, I hope because you thought of making use of them) Therefore, you should research areas near to you which you can donate the objects. Consider this: if something is no longer your style but that doesn't mean it's not suitable for anyone else.

If you're worried about giving away all your clothing (or perhaps you just need more cash) Consider the possibility of donating your garments to an thrift shop. Apart from earning money that you to buy something for yourself, or bears and coffee. You could can also:

...Will help make it easier for others to purchase good clothing (since the clothes are less expensive because they're used)

...Will be giving a second chance for your clothes to be given new owners who can actually take advantage of them - and will not keep them in the closet's back for months.

...Will help the local economy, as the majority of thrift stores are run locally by business proprietors.

When deciding whether to give away or visit an thrift store, be aware that there are charity thrift stores that collect funds to support social causes. The way it works is when you give your clothing and other accessories to a thrift store that is charitable which they then organize and sell them off, and they can aid a cause that is social, such as helping those in require it, supporting education projects, etc. It's a good use for those old clothing items.

Chapter 6: The Way To Skyrocket Communication Skills

Communication is something that no one will ever be able to take away from anybody. It will remain a major element of your daily life regardless of whether you'd like the idea or not. Since no one is an island, nobody could be without it. Without communication what are you going to get through your day-to-day life? What are the ways you'll be able to be able to learn what you need to? Without communication, the world is nothing but chaos.

Communication is the one thing that we all have to communicate our thoughts and ideas with other people. It's a way of introducing ourselves to other people and interacting in contact with them easily and freely. Communication is always that mysterious tool that connects all us throughout the years, and helps us discover brand new and unique things about each other and across the globe.

Talk

Communication is simply speaking about what you are saying and distributing it for people to listen, view or feel. There aren't many of us who are excellent speakers. That is the reality. However, every single one of us has the potential to become a great speaker. All we have to do is practice.

Try speaking to yourself in front of a mirror. you might use the mirror to say "hi there" or something. Make sure that nobody else is in the room as you as you practice this. If you're not sure what you should say to yourself in front of the mirror, take a look at the book. It will also help you feel more comfortable making your voice heard however, it will also help you control your voice tone, volume, and even the way you present your voice when you speak. It will also allow you to speak more clearly and increase your vocabulary.

People who struggle to talk are referred to as natural introverts. They cannot make themselves approach people at parties they've been forced to attend. These are the people who would like to connect with others but are scared to do an appearance or do something which would cause them to look odd or foolish. They are are too aware of what others might think of their actions. This isn't an issue you're able to solve for yourself.

It's not always possible for others to speak to you first. It is possible to start by making a comment about something they're wearing or are wearing. If you've already have met them in the past but haven't had the chance to have the same level, you can greet them by saying "Hi You're the one from the other party, aren't you?" This can lead to discussing what happened to the party, where they work , and the reason they got to where they are.

Be sure to start with a small amount, particularly if it is your first time to meet them. After you've greeted them with an opening, you can start by asking them about your interests or friends who are similar to them. Don't discuss the weather. It's the kind of topic that was rated as the least interesting, but the most popular topics of all time.

Try to play jokes at the right times. Be careful not to be overly enthusiastic as it might turn off your new acquaintances. You can share a few details about yourself, but not the most intimate details particularly to those you have only have met. If you can share something about yourself, it is sure to make them feel more comfortable sharing something about themselves also. Share interesting stories and be sure to identify your common interests and discuss it.

Make it a habit to ask open-ended questions when you're looking to engage in an interesting conversation. Beware of questions that can be answered with an 'yes' or "no" if you don't have any questions to follow up with your new friend. When you meet one in the beginning can be the most difficult part of the process however, you must present yourself in the best light and have fun doing it. Don't view it as a task but instead treat it as an opportunity to go to many other enjoyable night outs and hangouts!

Make use of your body

"Using the body" is a requirement to connect with your listeners or audience by using body movements, such as eye contact or basic hand movements.

Eye contact is an essential part of learning to communicate. When you stare straight into the eyes of someone you're speaking to gives genuine signals. Eye contact helps your audience members more attentive to the topic you're discussing. It will also allow you to discern if your listener is having fun or if your topic causes discomfort for the person listening. Naturally it will also give them the chance to scrutinize your behavior. Don't appear at them as bored, annoyed, or uninterested even if you're not really meaning it , as it could make them reconsider whether or not they are believing what you're telling them, or make them want to cut off the conversation right away.

Try smiling. Smiles can bring out your positive energy and lead to the possibility of a long and pleasant conversation. If, for some reason, you aren't able to do it easily, try practicing it before the mirror for about 10 minutes each day. It's a great exercise for your face and an excellent method of saying, "Hi! I'm nice!"

Make use of your hands to convey your thoughts. This will help your audience comprehend the message you want to convey. It can also help you appear more friendly and enjoyable to converse with since it is sometimes a way to open to a sudden joking exchange Be careful not to overstate when it's not needed and don't appear awkward.

Make sure your facial expressions, words and gestures are consistent as it may transmit mixed signals. For instance, you can't make a comment to someone when you're looking at them with a frown or scowl or appear as if you're making fun of them or are jealous. Allow your body to move with your thoughts and words.

If you're speaking in front of a large audience move around. But not all the time however, since it could cause discomfort for the audience. Move around the room as your presentation demands you to. This will help you to emphasize your message and get your audience involved more.

Pay attention

Being attentive helps you comprehend what people are saying and helps you respond more in a timely manner. This could lead to more conversations, while keeping the air more light. Being heard is an honor that every speaker should enjoy. Pay attention to the way you would like other people to be listening to you.

Don't think ahead about how to speak, without letting the speaker take the stage first. Don't interrupt. Many people are angry when other people do not pay attention to the things they say. Remove any distractions you can think of if that what the speaker has to say is significant. Remove your phone or laptop, or put aside your book to give them the opportunity to speak , and also allow yourself to gain knowledge. Keep your eyes on the ball.

Try to imagine yourself in the shoes of others when they confide their concerns to you. You can feel confident that they trust you enough to come over to you during difficult times. You must give him or her the necessary advice and physical security. The best way to know the best way to respond in such instances is to listen , and picture you are experiencing what the other person is experiencing.

Consider putting yourself in other person's position to understand his perspective.

It is important to be aware of when to end your listening. There are times when you need to do it, particularly when the subject is like an untruthful gossip, something that could hurt someone or unimportant and hinders your work. It is important be aware of when to tell a person to 'no however, you must be polite and firm in a calm tone.

Be You

When you do all of these things and letting go of the things you've been hiding behind your'shy mask, don't let go of a glimpse of who you are.

Be yourself. Don't be intimidated. Be confident about your skills as well as your thoughts and ideas. Take pride in your personal hobbies and meet people who appreciate and respect you in all aspects. Falsehood is not an answer, but rather adds to your existing issues.

Chapter 7: What To Start

We've discussed the advantages of downsizing, let's talk about the best way to go about it. It is easier to downsize when you're forced to or have to perform it. For instance, your landlord has sold the property you are renting and you must relocate to a smaller space. In this case, there is a deadline that must be adhered to. You have to leave within this time frame and you don't have the room to store all of your belongings. This creates a sense of need for urgency, and requires you to take choices. For some , it may be somewhat more difficult to reduce their size because they wish to. I've downsized at least once, and many think, "I wish I could do this." But they never actually do. Their backs aren't in the direction of the walls, therefore the idea is lost and they remain content in their inaction. I think they do not act because they believe it's an overwhelming job. There isn't a proper or incorrect way to downsize. I would suggest you should do what is most effective for you. So this section is specifically targeted towards those who want to reduce their size and aren't compelled to do so.

Start with your goal.

Note on a piece of paper your desire to become minimalist and downsize. This is essential. It is crucial in other areas that you live. If you don't write your goals down, it's not a goal. It is just a dream. The majority of people who do not record their goals don't achieve their goals.

Note down the reasons you would like to live a minimalist lifestyle. Create a list of the reasons you'd like to simplify your life. The more reasons you have, the more likely you'll succeed. This will motivate you to achieve your goal of decluttering and becoming a minimalist.

Create a realistic timeframe of when you'd like to complete the initial phase of downsizing. If you're reducing the size of your home or large amount of things then you'll need to break it into smaller deadlines. For instance, you could break it into rooms. You must, however, set a deadline. The feeling of urgency can make a difference. Once you are able to meet the deadlines you set, you'll get momentum and feel feelings of pride and satisfaction.

Consider the obstacles you'll be faced with when moving downsizing. What are you putting off? Are you limiting someone else in your children, or you alone? Most of the reasons that you will discover are internal. It is beneficial to acknowledge these reasons now, so you'll have the chance to conquer your internal battle.

Are you in need of any assistance in achieving your goals of downsizing? If you live with someone else, then of course you'll need their assistance. Do you have the ability to bring them aboard or request their help? If you are living by yourself it is possible to ask whether any of your acquaintances are willing to assist.

Make your downsizing plan together. It is here that you bring all the above into one. Write down what you need to accomplish first. Plan what you'll be doing in the next step and so on. Remember to establish deadlines and keep on track.

Every day, think of your target as if it had already been achieved. Imagine the feeling of fulfillment you'll feel when you are done. Continue to do this until you've achieved your goal of reducing the size of your home.

Be persistent. If you fail to meet the deadline make another deadline and then work towards reaching that new date. It is possible to accomplish so much by setting deadlines.

THE ACTION

Do not try everything at all at once. This can lead to failure. Think of it as a procedure. It's actually a process that, once you begin and continue, it can take forever. If you attempt to complete it with the "every room at once" approach, you're likely to be overwhelmed and eventually stop. Set an appropriate timeframe for actions. This will help ensure that you are on the right the right track and give you a feeling of urgency.

Begin in one room of your house. I would suggest starting with the room where you are spending the majority of your in your daytime hours. The reason I think this is because you'll notice results fast. After you've reduced the size of the space, you'll notice that you're less stressed and be more motivated to tackle the next space that you use the most time in.

Before you begin the process of de-cluttering things in a specific space, you should have an idea of what you intend decide to do with objects you're getting rid of. Do you donate the items to a local charity? You can sell them off on Craigslist? Toss them in the trash or recycle them? There will be multiple piles of garbage that you have to get these items from your house in the shortest time possible. I believe that the use of thick black garbage bags are useful. After you've decided that the item has to go place the item into the bag. You won't be able to see it and it makes it much easier. Be sure to trust me. Make sure that you make clarified what's trash and what items were used for other purposes.

Do you require the item or want to use it? Before you begin make sure to ask this question in your the back of your mind. It's easy however, once you begin cutting back, asking that question will assist you in developing the "flow". The flow will to give you the energy that you require to make the necessary changes. Change isn't easy in the world however, many times , it can be positive. I think you'll feel the process of reducing your size as empowering. You can do it!

What do you think of sentimental items? If you believe you're going to be regretting throwing the thing you're emotionalally attached to, into the garbage or charity, then don't. There are items that are meaningful to us. I'd never let go of that one object that has been in my family for more than 200 years. I think the issue is when we become emotionally attached to many objects, lots of them. Sometimes, we inherit or are gifted items by our loved ones who died. It's fine to treasure the objects, but do you believe they would like you to carry around those items. I am not able to speak for every one of your lost loved ones however I am certain they would want the items that meant something to them to be given to someone who would appreciate them as much as they do, instead of accumulating dirt in the house. The things that our loved ones have aren't their possessions. As I mentioned that downsizing is a process. You can keep the sentimental things in the present, but then decide to let them go once you're more settled. There are many different ways to look at things. Certain people are not willing to abandon these items Others take pictures of these items and store the pictures in an album and others donate objects. You can decide. I enjoy thinking about this possibility regarding the loved ones that I could leave behind. Do you want them to feel tied to or burdened by your belongings? Everyone has different answers.

Chapter 8: Minimalism At Work

The job situation is one that you have to deal with. You must work to earn a living however, there are options to bring this process towards a conclusion. If you are not able to find a chance of a new job that you'd like more than what you are doing today, you need to make an effort to lessen the effect that your job can have on your life. It might be that you feel overwhelmed or dissatisfied over the way you're treated by your colleagues. If you have an chance to change jobs to one you would like more and you are able to do it, then take advantage of it.

3. Sort through your workplace priorities

It is possible that, as an unsecure person, you've received praise from colleagues and count on it to feel confident about yourself. It's not a healthy method. If you're doing well in the job you perform it's enough to feel you've done a good job and you don't have to announce it. The people who appear to need praise won't ever be considered for top positions because they're not enough, therefore If you can rid yourself of this neediness, you'll be much more likely to receive an the honest evaluation that will allow you advance your career. The steps you must to reduce include:

Stop doing multiple tasks

Set what your objectives for today

Give work to people who are better than you.

Be sure to have a work-order that is simple

The majority of stress comes from having to handle more than a dozen tasks at once. It is possible to get those dozen tasks completed faster by dividing them up into priority and tackle each one at a time. If you have tasks such as this are urgent, they should be at the top of your list . the time of day when you first arrive at your workplace is the ideal time to tackle tough jobs because your brain power is at its best during this time of the day. If you're required to distract yourself from important work, make sure to ask politely whether someone else could do it since you're on the verge of an end date. Don't try to become the hero. The hero isn't necessarily the one who died by working too hard. The hero remains strong and is counted on.

As you set your objectives for the day be sure to assign them a certain duration of time. When it is done and you are ready to move onto the next project. You will discover that people are more reliant on you by taking on less work at a given time, and not be their"doormat. It is important to realize that it's not doing you any good to act this way. If you look at the top management, you'll see that it is rare for a manager is so busy there isn't enough time to oversee. If you're looking to be promoted it is best to be more efficient. That means you should complete the projects that you're assigned one at a given time and trying to beat yourself up to complete those tasks. Don't look for approval. Just be happy with your own pace and work to improve the speed as time goes by. When you accelerate your speed by remaining mono-dimensional and not multi-tasking you'll notice that that you are able to be trusted with more responsibility . You will be able manage it effectively because your minimalist method of working.

Clean your desk of clutter. Make a list of what you should keep in your workspace. Remove the distractions. We often overload our minds with cell phones,

phones, Internet connectivity and social media. Turn off. This is the perfect time to work. Make breaks as you need to, but when you're doing your work, count the time and strive to improve in what you can accomplish within a an allotted time. A lesser amount of distractions can assist you in doing this, and these are the distractions you must eliminate.

If you are a home-based worker and you work from home, it may cause stress in addition. You're trying to manage your personal life and your work schedule and sometimes the lines are crossed. You must be disciplined to work according to a set schedule similar to what you do at the office. If you have an area that is separate from your work This will be helpful as you are able to cut your mind off from the distractions and chaos of your house without feeling guilty for not doing your housework or not focusing on household duties. It is important to realize that you'll actually accomplish more when you are free of any distractions this will allow you more time with your family and engage in the things families are expected to spend time doing together.

It is important to take breaks, and, even if you work in a home-based environment plan your own breaks when you are able to be active and get moving and drink a glass of water. But, you should avoid using the internet during your work hours, even during breaks as this could draw you in and take up hours. If you decide to take breaks, do it for a specific time. The less clutter you have in your work space will make the work more enjoyable and provide more. Making sure that your workspace is organized and it's clean and well-organized isn't too difficult. You must put in the effort to make a space that inspires you, and then keep it tidy and clean to be able to return it clean at night, after your work is completed.

Chapter 9: De-Cluttering The Mind

I stated in the introduction that you could be among those who carry lots of emotional baggage in their life. This can hinder your work and makes you more dependent. If you've been snubbed for promotion and you find out that other people around you are receiving far more than frosting on the cake, there's probably reasons. If your mind is filled with thoughts or emotions and there's no opportunity for creativity and excitement and you're very dependent and don't seem to be the most desirable candidate that employers are able to choose. So, it's time for you to get rid of the clutter and make yourself less needy and less messy particularly in the area of emotions.

One of the most effective methods of decluttering the mind is by adopting the mindfulness posture. What that means, in a very simple way, is to remain in the present moment and are not focusing on events that have transpired, as they are gone, and they aren't able to come back. You don't think about the future. It's not yet happened and it isn't likely to take place. The issue with being directed to think this way is that they are resistant to the idea. The best method to help you get to adopt this method that you think is to commit an hour or two per day to meditation. It helps you to become more mindful, and when troubles occur throughout your day, you can return to your thoughts in the present to prevent getting sucked up with the jumble of daily life.

Meditation on mindfulness

Find a place within your home that you can enjoy 20 minutes of silence. It is important to dress in a comfortable outfit since your last desire want is to have your waistline getting hurt. You must be in a place where in a place where noise from outside is minimal. Relax your back and sit straight. The ideal chair to do is a chair that is hard such as a dining table, but do not lean to the side. It is important to maintain a straight back and your head slightly bent. This will open up your airways so that it is easier for the person to breath.

Keep your eyes shut during the first session as this will help you stop the mind wandering. Then, inhale through your nose to the number eight, and then exhale, focusing your attention focused on your breath only. Repeat the exercise. Be aware of the air entering your lung. Take a moment to be in the moment and then notice the air leave your body. What you're doing is taking in more air than usual, and this can help you tremendously since it implies that your sympathetic nervous system can deliver oxygen to all of the proper locations in your body, whereas it isn't able to effectively while you breath normally. While you are sitting and breathing and you notice that your mind is wandering and you are unable to focus, bring your thoughts back to the breathing. Don't be a victim of not being able to completely concentrate. It will take a while before you are in a position to do so as your mind is used to having lots of thoughts and thinking, and clearing it all out can take some time.

Keep doing this for around 20 minutes per day. Personally, I suggest you start in the early hours of morning prior to breakfast as this is a very peaceful moment. What you will discover after having practiced this for a few weeks is that it can help you through your day to everyday life. If an unfortunate event occurs or is unexpectedhappens, you are able to pause for a while to think of the solution instead of becoming stressed over it. This kind of meditation will make you aware of not allowing issues to become a source of stress. It improves your concentration also and makes you feel more calm. It also helps me realize that meditation can make me more productive as emptying my mind this way allows me to to keep things in my mental space that have more importance than thoughts that go unchecked.

I suggest that you practice it every day, and never attempt to do it before eating. It is also important to ensure that you allow your body enough time to rise from your the meditation to get back to your day, as this type of practice can lower your heart rate and blood pressure. It requires a bit of time to return to normal after breakfast. If you are overwhelmed at work, take a deep breath this way and allow the present moment to be what you focus on, since it will assist you to discover solutions that can be effective. It will also be evident that you be more mindful of your health when your mind is not filled, rather than being able to open all those boxes constantly, causing you to be less productive.

Sometimes you need to let yourself become the child in you. If you're planning to leap into the puddle and splash around and splash, it's well to do it. If you're looking to laugh at things with your children it can be beneficial as you let the brain part which is involved in creativity to have some breathing room. When they conducted scans of Buddhist monastery monks that meditated they discovered that there was equally utilized the creative and logic part of the brain. this reduces stress and reduce the ways external influences affect your life and allows you to become as productive as you're supposed to be.

Chapter 10: Devise A New System Or Organization

If you are able to clear rooms in your home and you can look at the basic structure of your home. This will help you decide what style you prefer to follow. The organization helps you maximize your time off and makes life less of a hassle. For instance how much time do you typically devote to cleaning your house? If you establish the new rule that you always clean a room the way it was when you first entered it, you can reduce your time and make your home a more comfortable place to live in. This allows you to unwind and relax when you're at home, and it also allows you time for the most enjoyable activities that life offers, like being more social with your friends and family, as well as having the ability to locate items when you require they are needed.

Katy's house was filled with charts everywhere. There was one for her children and one for her schedule and vacation times as well as birthdays, and another for appointments with a dentist and dental. The charts were scattered all over the home. There was another in the bathroom, so she could track her weight. In the present day you can organize all this information onto your iPad or phone and then make it available to anyone who requires it. This reduces the quantity of clutter within your home.

Also, become accustomed to filing your documents. The only document I have at home that can be accessed by opening the file itself is one which isn't taken care of. When it's completed and filed, I make sure to file it. It may sound like a chore however, once you are familiar with living this manner, your house is more organized and your expenses are up-to-date. It's easier to remember things, and it removes a lot of anxiety out of your daily life. It is the most important aspect of minimalistic living.

In this tiny picture, you can visualize what happens when implement minimalism in your daily life. In this space there's nothing that's unnecessary. Everything is put away once it's done but moving from one area to the next lets light be flooded into the house. There's the fireplace. It has artwork however the owner has cleverly used smaller pieces to make more. Imagine if artwork were your thing. If you were to introduce art that was colored in an interior layout like this, the eyes would be drawn straight to the bright color, and it creates the artwork as the main central point for the entire room. Every room in the home should be an element that is the central point of interest, whether it is a photographs of family members or the overall dimensions and the size of the space. A minimalist home is easier to maintain and has enough storage space since the homeowners do not have a lot of items. The things they do own are well-organized and can easily locate them and makes a significant difference in the layout and the function of the home. People who realize that what advertisements are promising to do isn't doing them any good by providing them with items that they don't need, want, or desire.

Your organization must extend to how you live your life. The simple act of changing some bad habits to positive ones will benefit the organisation. For instance, if you're being surrounded by negative people decide to eliminate the ones who don't contribute any value to your daily life. Minimalism can be applied to any area of your life. Why let those who do not like you to hinder your life? Also, if your home life is well-organized then follow that same pattern in your professional life. This gives you more time for yourself and makes the entire life process much more enjoyable.

Get your wildest side nature

Did you think being minimalist meant boring? Really, it's not. Imagine a room that's white. Imagine opening the doors to discover you are able to see that French doors open to an outdoor area that allows one to be near to the natural world. It's a beautiful effect and could make your home appear as larger while also encouraging the homeowner to stay in nature that will help to reduce the burden on your shoulders when it comes to stress. Scientists have proven that spending time in nature will improve your mental state and when you allow this aspect of your nature the space to grow and expand and expand, you are able to re-engage with the most important aspects of your life and make decisions that will can help you transition from the world of consumption and towards self-sufficiency. Okay, you don't have the time to grow your own food and at the cost they are available in the market so why would you make your life more complicated. Living in a area that transforms into an outdoor space doesn't need to be difficult work. Just a few well-placed plants, perhaps an evaporative feature, and some effective lighting, and your overall home experience will go up an notch.

It's not obvious until you attempt it. The most effective way to proceed is to adhere to the tips for decluttering in this chapter and the other chapters. Minimalist living is the process of reducing everything, which includes depression and stress and possessions. Also, it means maximising what little you have within your daily life. Keep in mind that "Less can be a of a lot more."

Chapter 11: Eliminating Of Clutter, Excess Stuff, And Sentimental Items

As I've mentioned before the concept of minimalism doesn't just revolve around eliminating physical objects, though that's an excellent starting point! But be patient before you rush into your closet to throw away everything. We all know how to go about it when it comes to cleaning out the clutter. It could be as easy as auctioning off all the things stored in the garage, but we will explore more of the subject in the future.

The Why

The main reason to declutter in the context of minimalism is to understand the reason i.e. the reason you are decluttering it in addition to the rewards you receive following. If you get up in the morning and toss things away without having a reason in mind as to why you're doing it, you'll not feel content and satisfiedfor longer term, at the very least. The reasons behind it can be more mysterious than the process since it is individual and unique to you. Ask yourself the following questions:

What are the reasons I would like to go minimalist?

Does it have to do with the fact that minimalism is in fashion or do I would like to simplify my life?

Who would I like to be?

What do I envision my life to be?

What's it that concerns me?

What is the reason I don't feel fulfilled?

Each of these questions has no simple answer. But when you're looking to reduce your clutter, it is essential to be clear, and it is essential to know the answer to each one of these questions. Be sure to understand why minimalism is essential in your life and the goals that you hope to achieve through being one.

The How

After you have your reasons set then you can concentrate on your what. To get rid of clutter, you can utilize a variety methodsthat work best for you. A few of the most popular are:

The Dive-In Approach

Packing Party

Four Box Method

The Dive-In Approach

It's as easy as renting the dumpster, removing everything, and beginning a new path new life that is more satisfying. This is ideal for those who plan to RV (living in a motorhome (RV)) that is a standard minimalist activity. What better way to get rid from the material world than living in a home that you are moving.

Although this approach is as simple as it may sound, it can be quite challenging, especially for those who are just beginning to learn about minimalist. It's true that letting go of the things you've owned throughout your life isn't easy.

A Packing Party

This method, developed by the Minimalists is a moderate method of decluttering your house. A packing event involves packing your possessions as if you were moving. If I refer to everything I am referring to everything, including bathroom and furniture.

Label each box so that if you ever need something, you will be able to locate it. Once you're finished, you can spend the next three weeks (or longer) simply removing the items you actually use i.e. the things that add value to your life. After 3 days (or more) have passed, you can donate or sell the rest of the objects that are still inside the containers.

Apart from being labor intensive This method is also incredibly effective because it will assist you in getting rid of things you do not need. It is not likely to miss what's in the boxes away from sight and out of your mind. In addition, if you are thinking of moving, this strategy could be the most effective option you can choose. Take all the boxes to your new home and then take 3 weeks to unpack only what you require.

Four Box Method

This method involves separating the clutter into boxes that are that are labeled as put away, give away, toss away and undetermined. Find clutter in your home and throw it into the appropriate category, then sort each box according with the labels. With the undecided boxes, this technique allows for some flexibility in case you're not sure of what to do with it yet.

This is a simple and simple, however problems could arise when more items begin getting piled in the undecided box. It is best to avoid placing items in the box unless you're uncertain about something.

There are various other ways to clean your house however, you don't need to follow any specific method. You can also opt to get rid of just one thing per day or just one thing on the first day or the first day of the month. and two items on day two , and the list goes on. Decide how you would like to declutter because minimalism is a way to live your life in peace.

Deleting Specifics When Clearing

To become minimalist, it is important to consider typical items that we must all cut back on. These include things like books, decor, clothes as well as furniture. It can help to know how to handle each one of them separately.

A minimalist's outfit

Consider putting together an outfit that is a staple, that is essentially a collection of timeless and well-made items that are able to be mixed and worn for any occasion. Therefore, it's best to stay with the latest trends that reflect your personality. The basic idea is:

If you've not used it within a year, you need to replace it.

If you're planning to keep it for a future time e.g. after losing weight, you can let it go.

If it doesn't make you feel confident about yourself every time you put it on, take it off.

If someone borrowed one of your clothes and do not come back, get rid of them and you'll be okay if they didn't return.

It doesn't mean you'll never buy clothes. It's just that you have the option to buy clothes, but not due to pressures. It is possible to choose shades like gray, black or white which can be worn in various ways and you don't need to think about whether you're wearing something that matches.

A minimalist's decor

Pinterest and inspiring Instagram accounts , aside from minimalism, it doesn't need your walls to be empty or your tables to be entirely empty. They're usually empty due to the fact that it's difficult to locate something meaningful to hang upon your walls.

If you plan to hang something on your wall ensure it has meaning to you or represents something that you value. If you plan to put items on your dining table, make sure it be a present from someone that is meaningful to you or that makes you smile when you come across it. Everything else is fine.

The Minimalist's Books

I understand that creating your own library can be appealing, but unless a book has was a real inspiration to you that you'd like to read it or refer to it over and over again, it's going to have to be thrown away. There are books you may have (that you have no intention to go through) that could be used by someone else that aren't able to purchase books, and could change their lives for the better. Donate it today!

You can save the books that changed you the way you think, your childhood books or books you'd like to gift to your children, etc.

Always looking for books. You might also decide to buy yourself an library card or, even better you can get to the Kindle version.

A minimalist's Furniture and Utilities

In the case of furniture, your primary concern must be on their value above all other considerations. If you find that something isn't serving any purpose, you should eliminate it.

In the case of kitchenware and utility items the golden rule is to do not put anything in multiples. One baking sheet or frying pan If you have a large family, have utensils available to serve them all- not more and no less. If you take care of and wash them after every use, they'll suffice.

To be used for Sentimental Items

Everyone has these. The faded letters, the Post cards, stuffed animals They all bring us back to a moment or a person an area. This is among the main obstacles in the transition to minimalism. Don't be fooled sentimental things aren't good and keeping these items isn't a bad thing.

But, the risk of sentimental items is more nimble. Although it may be difficult to acknowledge it, sentimental objects burden you in some way or another. Do you remember the most recent time you were through such things. If it didn't have a negative impact on your body, then you're one of the hardcore ones.

If you're keeping something because of sentimental reasons, it's time to relieve yourself from the weight. Let go of items that are sentimental is best accomplished through the all-in or dive-in method to avoid retracing your steps.

The most important thing to remember is that memories aren't stored in physical objects but within your brain. Whatever symbolise the memory, that is what it really is, a symbol but not a memory. Therefore, it's fine not to hold onto it.

Note that you don't have to eliminate everything sentimental, but If something is bringing you genuine happiness, then you can take it home and keep it!

After you have eliminated everything unnecessary within your personal life, it's time to rid yourself of relationships that are toxic. We will discuss it in the following chapter.

Chapter 12: Preparing For The Change

Depending on the place you are in the realm of collecting or hoarding items the change may be quite painful for you. Thus, prior to starting the process, you must physically and mentally get ready for this significant changes that are about to occur. With that in mind let's look at how you can mentally prepare yourself to letting go of your habits of hoarding and physically collect the tools you'll require to accomplish this.

Mental Preparation

If you purchase this book and absorbing the advice that are contained in the book, you've already made a significant step towards a bright, free of clutter. But it does not necessarily mean you're prepared to let go of the things you need to do to get rid of this unpleasant habit.

Take some time to think about how you can prepare yourself mentally. You should be able to identify what you think could be the cause of this condition.

As we have discussed in Chapter One, it is possible that you might feel lonely or feeling unsatisfied. If you're not successful in determining the cause of your issue, you might consider confiding your concerns to a trusted person or a family member, and ask them to help you determine the issue.

Once you've finished take a moment to list the things that you've kept and then consider what purpose they serve in your daily life. There is a good chance that they will have no practical reason for them, or even purely for sentimental reasons there isn't any sentimental attachment to many of the objects you've accumulated over the decades. It is likely that once you start going through the items you will discover items that you've completely lost track of and which have no significance at the moment you made the decision to save it. If you are able to see that the items you've kept have no significance, you will be able to move on with the items.

When your brain starts to think of reasons the reason for something's worth You must force yourself to evaluate the truthfulness of these assertions. Are those ripped-up underwear pieces that you put on in the past when you broke your vows is really all that important? Perhaps it's something that's not just taking up space in your cupboard and could be the cause of a health risk. It's the same for the pile of newspaper that is that are piled up on your sofa. Instead of dwelling upon the past, you should consider that a real living person might be sitting there at times, while you get to know each other better. We'll go over specific items in greater detail in the following chapter, however, for now, you need to accept the fact that you'll be shedding the majority of your possessions. The best way to go about it is to recognize that they don't serve any value and that's why you're holding the items for no reason.

This can be one of the most anxious one, so it might be beneficial to consume herbal teas or alternative ways to ease your mind and keep your focus to the task at time without worrying about it excessively.

Physical Preparation

If you've thought about letting yourself go mentally, it can allow you in obtaining the tools you'll need to complete the cleaning of your home.

If you are not absolutely required, limit your shopping to these items:

Garbage bags

Recycling bags (to separate garbage from recycling)

Rubber gloves or latex (choose one)

Zip-ties

Cleaning equipment (only if you don't already have them)

These items will assist you in your cleaning task and will make it easier for you to dispose of large amounts of things.

It is vital to not purchase more than the items listed on the list above , unless you are absolutely required. Keep in mind that you're trying to rid yourself of things, not add additional items. If you don't trust you to avoid buying unnecessary items or services, you can ask someone else to take care of it for you. It's only a temporary option, but as you'll need to eventually take care of yourself, and you will learn to not allow yourself to desire to purchase items that aren't really needed.

The process of preparing yourself, particularly physically and mentally (resisting the desire to not overspend) is one of the most challenging steps you make on the road towards self-improvement. However, once you have completed this step your tasks will be more labor demanding, not stress-inducing. If you've successfully completed this step, great job! We will then take a look at the actual things within your home and discover how to sort them , and begin the actual process of disposing. Don't stop now You've been doing a fantastic job to date. Continue to work hard!

Chapter 13: Learn About The Minimalist Lifestyle

A lot of people live in a chaotic life. They own too many things that they don't use. People are obsessed numerous things and being too busy in general. Even though they're not content in their current lives they're scared to simplify them and aren't willing to live a minimalist lifestyle for fear that it could destroy all things that are worth taking care of. But it's not going to happen. A minimalist lifestyle is about adding enjoyment in your daily life and not taking it away.

There is no need to provide well-crafted objects.

The rule of thumb is that quality should prevail over quantity. For instance, if you own three pairs of high-quality shoes that you actually wear, and a hundred pair of uncomfortable, cheap shoes, you should get rid of the ones that aren't worth your money. You'll have more space, and picking out footwear will be faster and more enjoyable to choose, and you'll not be embarrassed when you look at the high-heeled shoes and sandals that seemed nice when you purchased they did not last long, and then gave you blisters the only time you used them, or didn't turn out to match to your outfit.

You shouldn't be forced to sacrifice tasty food either.

Certain minimalists are vegetarians or vegans. Some don't. The concept of minimalism can be used in any way. Certain people opt for simple, basic meals. Others continue to enjoy elaborate meals. Again, the minimalist lifestyle is a good choice. The goal is to manage the amount of food you consume and not worry about the preparation. If you are a fan of cooking complex meals, then by all means, do it! If you'd rather cook food that is simple and tasty rather than something complicated and delicious it's the ideal choice. People who are minimalists tend to eat natural foods and steer clear of processed foods however, it's still delicious meals.

There's no need to be like monks

While some choose to be monks or Spartans however, many people don't. Do you enjoy your comfortable furniture? So, keep it insofar that it doesn't obstruct your living space, as the goal is to clear your home, not lay upon the ground.

Your friends will not be angry at you.

There are those with a skepticism about anyone who doesn't behave in the same way as they do. This is a sign that they are suspicious of the vast majority of humanity as even people from the same nation don't follow the same path. If you do have family members or friends with similar characteristics when they realize that you're not trying to make them change their lifestyles and lifestyles, they'll embrace the change within your own.

There's no need to be a minimalist as (insert the name of a well-known minimalist of your choice)

All minimalists are not alike. There are those who reside among deserted islands, or even in the middle of nowhere. Others reside in major cities such as New York or London, and yes, they are employed and have cars as well as big apartment or houses, and have large families. The goal of a minimal lifestyle is that you create a an easy way of living that fits your lifestyle and lifestyle choices that are not like the others.

The minimalist lifestyle isn't threatening or unusual. It's a way of life where you only own things that you actually need and utilize to complete tasks that actually have to be done which means you have time, space, and energy to focus on what's truly essential to you.

There are pros and Cons of Minimalist lifestyle

It is crucial to understand why a minimalist decides to lead a minimalist lifestyle. There are some misconceptions regarding minimalist living, and this is the reason why some societies think that minimalist living is designed for the older generation. However, there should be good reasons for people to decide whether or not be living this way. Let's examine the advantages and disadvantages of living a minimalist life.

The Cons

We've been raised with plenty of competition beginning at home as well as our schools and then into our work environments. The culture has taught us to always strive to climb up the ladder, not sacrificing the height of the ladder if we can succeed.

According to Abraham Maslow's theory of human needs, the most important level that an individual could attain after having surpassed all other levels is self-actualization. However, this trend is beginning to change; people need more than just self-actualization-they want more stages to be added in that theory so that they can even be more self-actualized. This is the reason why society will continue to provide their children with education regardless of the rising unemployment rate into the economic system. It is the goal for every parent: a quality education and the most rewarding job for your child.

The Pros

Minimalists behave as they do due to the fact that they were raised in this way. For instance, if you grew up in a home that is vegetarians, it does not necessarily mean that you're less than slender because you aren't allowed to take meat. Your family was raised in a way that isn't a problem and there are no excuses for it.

In addition, minimalists want to live in a clutter-free space. For instance, a smaller house with a larger family requires clearing out. Instead of adding more things in a smaller house A minimalist would prefer to reduce the amount of stuff that can bring happiness as well as calm. In addition they are interested in buying items that will last. The quality of the item isn't an issue if the item will last. It is possible to ask why they doing this? They definitely don't wish to fill their homes with unnecessary clutter. What would you do with a house that has an excessive amount of worn-out items cluttering up your home?

Then, minimalists would like to reduce the number of items they manage. There's no need to keep more than six vehicles in the parking area even if you could only use only one.

**

If you're considering how to get started on the minimalist way it's a good idea to consider what minimalism means to you.

What's your purpose?

Do you want to decrease the number of items that you have?

Are you able to cherish the things you cherish?

Do you want to live a an easy life while spending more quality time with your children?

Are you looking to be peaceful in your atmosphere and is it also a combination of all the above?

It's not something you can achieve in a single day, but it is changing your lifestyle and habits to be more aware of the environment around you and the impact you make on the planet. It's about reducing your waste and changing your behaviour as an individual consumer.

A minimalist lifestyle is about getting rid of or storing things you don't require or use and eliminating the excess things and not purchasing more!

Chapter 14: The Minimalist Makeover - Getting Started

Even though your minimal transformation does not need to appear as dramatic as those stories that were discussed in the previous chapter, they ought to have helped you realize that there isn't a "one size will fit all" solution to a minimalist life style. Making the change is about choosing what can help you rid your home of clutter and your mind rather than the life and thoughts of others. It is possible to get inspired by the story of another's minimalist style however, you don't need to follow exactly what they did in order to attain peace or to be regarded as minimalist. There's no point in making comparisons to the journey of any other. If you decide to approach it your way, the important thing is to take the necessary changes to improve your life.

Before you begin opening closets and throwing out clothes like a madman There are a few steps to do to prepare the transformation of your home. This includes changing your perspective to an esthetic perspective and getting your household members or family members to participate with the transformation process.

Change Your Mindset to Accept Minimalism

You might think that you've already adopted the idea of minimalism or else, you wouldn't be going through this book or deciding to transform your house. But, in order for the transformation to be as efficient as it can be and to keep from creating an even bigger mess than that with which you started It might be helpful to make some additional mental plans.

Minimizing Environmental Impact

Before you throw things around randomly it is important to establish a strategy in your mind of what you'll plan to do with the items that you do not keep. For the most part, minimalist folks are an environmentally-conscious crowd. There is no requirement that you become a granola maker, hemp-wearing farmer and begin growing yourself your food. But, it's not a bad idea for to think about the impact on the environment that comes from your choices during the journey to reduce your carbon footprint and even more.

So, how can you go about this process in the most environmentally-friendly way possible? by embracing the notions of recycling and reusing, obviously. Instead of throwing away anything you don't want to keep, think about alternatives. You can first donate a variety of items to second-hand shops. A lot of them are nonprofits which donate their profits to those who are in need. Also, it is possible that somebody else could be able to make a profit from your junk items.

Be aware that you could have family members or friends who might need your old toys as well. Children are typically delighted to receive gifts from their parents such as books, clothing, and books for their children. Many women, particularly adults are drawn to sifting through other's clothing and accessories in the hope of finding something they're in a position to wear or utilize.

When something that you do not require no longer is worth giving away, think about leaving it on your front lawn or next to a dumpster. Do not leave it on a day when you collect trash and it could end up getting taken to the dump. Instead, place it there for people to see while they're through your neighborhood or planning to dump their garbage. There are many who have a passion of recycling other people's antique furniture, decorations, clothes and other junk. Don't be shocked if, someday, you find your old kitchen chair turned into a planter for flowers and adorning someone's front lawn! This is an excellent method to reduce how much clutter that is in your living space and also encouraging the eco-friendly lifestyle of recycling household items.

In addition, when you're faced with the items you aren't able to offer for donation or to reuse or reuse attempt to recycle as many things as you can. In addition to the items that are commonly recycled that the trash collection service collects learn about other things can be recycled in your community. Electronic equipment that is old, such as cellphones, computer parts cords, damaged light bulbs can be recycled at various electronics stores in the world's industrialized. It is possible to conduct a bit of online research to find companies which will safely recycle or dispose of furniture and appliances that are no longer used for you. Many disposal firms will pay you cash for various kinds of scrap metal in furniture and appliances, too.

Consider throwing things to the trash as a last resort to disposing of unwanted items. If there's no way to donate, offer recycling, reuse, or repurpose the object, ensure the item is removed with as green a method as you can. If it's biodegradable ensure that you dispose of it in a biodegradable container. If it is contaminated with any material, you must to find a firm who disposes from it in a secure manner for you.

Easy Does It

As eager and elated you are to begin this transformation and completed, keep in mind that it isn't an easy task. It's about to be an extensive overhaul of your house and your the way you live. If you speed it up, it might result in an interim change due to the fact that you didn't do enough thorough. Therefore, take your time and be patient when making choices. Be as deliberate and thoughtful as you can during the process of makingover, to ensure that you know the reasons behind every decision to either keep or throw away some thing.

Do not let yourself feel overwhelmed by the amount of work to do as you start your simple home renovation. Instead, work on developing tunnel vision. You should concentrate on one room at one time. In the room, you should concentrate on one cabinet. Then, only 1 drawer at a. In the end you'll be amazed the progress you've made. Instead of seeing it as just a race that has the goal of finishing, remember that you're on an ongoing journey. You'll continue to grow your knowledge of minimalism and how it relates to your daily life throughout the time you remain alive, so you could decide to settle down and set a pace that is comfortable for you and have fun.

Living a Life that is Begining to Have Purpose

One of the primary ideas that drives an approach to minimalism revolves around the concept of living your life with purpose or with a purpose. Instead of buying a bunch of things that are useless, just to the purpose of having them and enjoying them for a short time it is best to change your perspective to one of consciousness. Every time you decide on what to buy or how you will use on your own time or which place you'll go, it's best to make the decision in a mindful awareness of the motivation behind your decision.

If you are a minimalist every time you purchase something, it must be in line with a certain goal or purpose that has importance to you. If you're buying food items, consider your motives for every item you buy. Think about whether it will benefit your health or hinder it. Be aware of whether you purchased the product due to flashy marketing or its intrinsic nutritional benefit. Examine whether you already have something that is similar (but it might require some more planning on your behalf) at home. You could save dollars by not purchasing this item in the first place.

Although you're only in the beginning of your minimalist change the right time to begin taking action with intention is now.

Instead of spending your time with meaningless events and insignificant actions, begin to think about your goals and values and incorporate your heart into every choice you make, both big as well as small.

Prepare to Ask the Tough Questions and Answer honestly

The various phases of your home renovation will require you to sort your possessions into piles. In general you should divide items into three piles: one pile of items you will most likely keep the rest of your possessions, one pile that you won't keep, and a third "maybe" collection of things you're not sure.

While sorting your belongings, it is important to be prepared to ask to some truthful questions regarding every object. These questions include:

Does it really matter?

Does it bring value to my life?

What has the latest time that I was using it?

Why am I getting it?

Do I hold on to this item due to not achieving my objectives?

Do I hold on to this object due to an idealized image of me that is no longer in existence or was never there in the first time?

What does this item do to affect my feelings about myself?

How long am I contemplating using this item, or keep the item "just in case" and never making use of it?

If you are able to think about these questions and answer them in complete sincerity, you'll be able to drastically reduce the amount of things that are in"the "maybe" pile.

Choose the Best Place to Start

The book guides you through the rooms of your home beginning with what the authors believe as the most simple rooms to clean and minimize before moving on to some of the more difficult areas to work on. But, everyone has their own opinions or view of the best place to start and the final decision is yours.

There is a possibility that you are feeling overwhelmed by a specific section of your house and you may think that it is easier when you tackle this part first. However you could be overwhelmed by the areas you believe will be the most difficult to tackle, and would prefer to tackle these areas by beginning with simpler tasks. The order you get rid of clutter is your choice, so you decide to begin without delay. Make a list of the order that is the most logical to you and then go with the one you like best. If you're required to modify your strategy to accommodate changes and you need to change it, that's okay too. It's a flexible procedure. It is possible to move between chapters as often as you'd like.

It might help but at least pinpoint the areas in your home that you consider as the most stressful and chaotic. Take a list of the rooms in your home and arrange them in order of how much effort required to clean each. Be sure to include storage and closet spaces. If you're ready begin minimizing, choose whether you'll start with the easiest or difficult areas, and proceed through your list in the direction of your choice.

Involving Other Household Members

If you're living alone or with pets You are fortunate in this scenario. There is no reason to attempt to bring other people along with your minimalistic efforts. It is also not necessary to live in harmony with someone who doesn't desire to embark on a minimalism journey with you. You will not have to be able to make compromises between two distinct styles of living. The decision-making process is entirely up to you and you won't be required to ask for permission to throw away the item you want to throw away.

If you are living with families or roommates it is essential to include them in the minimization process. There are a variety of levels of involvement that household members, your significant other and even other family members could be at ease, and you need to be prepared to deal with any possible reactions to your minimalist thoughts and your efforts.

Many of you might already have decided to start this journey with a significant partner or roommate and both of you are prepared to embark on the whole journey together. But, you have to be aware that there could be a point at which you and your partner have different opinions on what objects to keep and what to get rid of. If this happens take care to treat the other's thoughts and feelings with respect. Don't force them to let go of things to which they've emotional connections and resist the temptation to argue or debate your position in a way that is excessively. You can rationally explain the reasoning behind your decision however, do not push your argument to the point of conflicting opinions. Don't allow yourself to be angry if your spouse would like to keep a possession which you consider worthy of keeping. Be aware that their minimalist path is just as important as yours, and you should accept that their method of living may differ from yours.

There are some of you who believe you have to convince your roommates, family members, or friends to join in this endeavor. Take care in this regard. There are many who do not accept a minimalist lifestyle, and it is important to be mindful of your neighbors' opinions and needs. The last thing you wish to do is dictate your lifestyle to them and then for them to begin to dislike you and minimalism.

If your household members aren't convinced to be a part of this process You are free to clearly and calmly explain the advantages of minimalism which are discussed in Chapter 1. It is also possible to share the anger you've experienced due to the pressure of being overwhelmed by clutter, having numerous possessions, and paying too much while you seek to live a life of meaningless of consumption. There is a good chance that they'll be able to identify with the majority of your experiences. They could decide on their own they want to get rid of the belongings they own or join in to join in minimising the home.

It is vital that you don't set any particular expectations for your housemates' participation in the process, or any enthusiasm to become minimalist. Resentments that are not met can cause resentment minimalism is about creating value in you life and avoid creating conflict. Take note of any amount of decluttering they opt to undertake on their own. Also, show appreciation for them understanding the need to make your life easier.

Here are some suggestions to go through the simple makeover, even if your friends don't want to participate in the process:

Respect your belongings. You may request politely to keep your belongings in their individual space or provide a space within shared storage that they may utilize as they please.

If you share space with others, like the dining room, bathroom and kitchen, inform the owners of any modifications you'd like to make prior to making changes. If they are not happy then ask them to assist in negotiating the best compromise.

Accept the fact that you won't always get everything you want for the whole home.

If you are looking to get rid of the property that is shared, request permission. Then give them the chance to keep the object (whatever it is) in their space, or propose an arrangement for where to put it.

In the event that you are in charge of your property and they rent the space, any modifications to the space you share are your option unless your lease says that otherwise. But, you must respect their wishes and not create an atmosphere that is uncomfortable or hostile for them.

If they keep insisting to leave their belongings scattered in the shared space, try to find some creative solutions for them, like a shelves for their belongings. Be considerate when explaining your desire to keep things in order and simple and don't criticize or devalue them.

The most important thing to maintaining peace in your living space is to respect one the other's views and wishes!

Special Tips on Participation of Children

In the event that you've got children that reside with you You have the chance to help them understand the advantages of minimalism even though they're still young. This might seem like an overwhelming task, as most children are borderline hoarders from the beginning. They love to keep intriguing odds and ends and build endless collections of similar objects and proudly display their memories from their most memorable moments in life, as well as squeeze all their belongings within their small rooms. As parents such children, they could be a source of constant discontent, but they could be inspiring in the sense that they see value in even the smallest of items.

As a parent, you have the final say on the things that are kept within your home and the objects are to be discarded. However, you should be careful not to irritate your children or force them into becoming minimalists. The resentment that comes from this type of behavior could lead to anger and adversely affect your relationship for a long time to in the future.

An effective method of engaging kids in the simple transformation is to present the benefits and advantages of this style of living in a manner that will appeal to the attention of your children. You can make it an enjoyable experience by following any and all these tips in accordance with the ages of your children.

Remember the enjoyment they've had playing with the toys they've owned for a number of years. Ask whether they would like to share their joy by donating their toys to children that might appreciate the toys.

Discuss the new lifestyle the basis of which you're embarking. Inform them that you're exhausted and stressed by being overwhelmed by too many things and you're trying to save cash for travel or for their higher education in the future. Children are often able to comprehend more than we do and may be very willing to accept your reasoning.

Then, challenge them to fill an empty box in the size that is yours to decide, with clothing and toys they no longer need or need.

Positively reinforce your child's efforts by saying things such as, "See how much easier it is to find items right now?" or "See how much more room you have to play in your space right now?"

Inform them they'll take much less time to tidy their rooms if they aid by getting rid of as much items as they can. This will allow them to have the chance to spend more time outside and play with their toys, or hang out with their acquaintances.

One of the benefits of living a minimalist lifestyle is to make less purchases in the near future for birthdays, as well as during Christmas. It is possible to help them comprehend the change in lifestyle by explaining that now you'll be able to save money to go on fun family vacations that you'll be going on. Don't make promises you can't keep, however.

Instead of buying a pointless amount of gifts for them ask them to reflect on the things they would rather have than anything. There is a good chance that they'll treasure the one or two things that matter to them much over a multitude of useless presents. If you teach children to value gifts for the meaning behind them , instead of looking at the value of material things, you are aiding in shaping them to be kind, non-materialistic kids.

If your children are very young, you might be able to complete every change without being aware or even not even. If this is your situation then you're lucky. But, regardless of the age of the children in your family, now you have the chance to inspire future generations to be more mindful of the environment, more deliberate when they make decisions and less materialistic their parents.

Ready Set, Go!

Once you've made some of the practical and mental preparations now is the time to start! The next chapter will cover the spaces that are common to living rooms, family and dining rooms. Feel at ease to skip any chapter that's pertinent to the beginning point of your minimalist overhaul. Happy decluttering!

Chapter 15: Benefits Of Minimalistic Living

Your attachment robs you of your freedom.

The system we live is a force for us to

Produce, work, with the aim of

Consuming, wearing more clothes, more phone

S, more vehicles, and even more houses. This is what

"The genius" is what Kiyosaki defines the term as "The Rat" which Kiyosaki defines as "The

race." So that the value of our race and our

the state of mind is conditioned to the

number of possessions we own. Huge

mistake. While I was in Bali I made the intention of visiting Bali, I made a

the backpack that weighs 6 kgs on my back I realized that my backpack was 6 kilos heavy.

the absurdity of having the number of

things. The greatest benefit of

The concept of minimalism is freedom. might seem

Strange and bizarre, but the more we own, the more

We are not as free as we think. It's simple.

Everything we own makes us feel secure.

If we collect many things we'll have

more pressing issues and should we do lose a gr

If it is damaged or is damaged, we have to replace it or replace it

Something new is able to replace it. This

results in frustration and discontent.

But, those living with less

We are so afflicted by material possessions. It's

Another advantage of minimalism

Therefore, I recommend you practice detaching.

You must be aware that living in a smaller space is not a good idea.

Does not mean that you're less, but it does mean being more liberated.

Your possessions shouldn't be the sole factor in determining

Your level of happiness. There's an amount of happiness that you can achieve.

false sense of well-being that we don't feel well

Buy something.

A

Pleasant

sensation

of

Acquiring

Something new and exciting that we like will likely to happen.

In a drawer, it was stored for the space of a couple of days. This

sense of satisfaction following the purchase

The effect is diminished as the hours pass. It's like feeling

ephemeral novelty. After a short time,

The sensation creates the sensation of a vacuum

since nothing is likely help us.

Problems or irritations.

A lot of people are very wealthy in

Material possessions and money are a part of

In the last stage of their lives, the

the deep emptiness been felt throughout the.

And , if we take one extreme suppose we were to have

Nothing at all, we'd not have

most liberating freedom to do and be.

What we want. Because of my

In my business, I'm always involved in this

There, and I understand the importance of

A minimalistic lifestyle, but definitely the

the benefits of minimalism start to be appreciated

When you practice it, and get the hang of it

Attachment bsurdity.

Minimalism is a way of life which consists of

living in a smaller space with fewer possessions. Also,

This, in turn, results in this, in turn, leads to.

Start with removing materials

Things, a set of stimuli appear in your mind,

Freedom, simplicity, and joy.

Minimalism is incorporated into your brain

as an exercise that is healthy. It is a good idea to start reducing,

Then, the negative thinking and the motives for

anxiety and stress. and everything else.

It becomes easier. It's then that you

Enjoy the benefits of minimalism

your life. There are people who believe that

the more we accumulate, the more satisfied we are. And

The truth is that a lot of objects are enslaving us

and force us to be afraid of and losing

They. The most appealing feature of the minimalist style is that it's easy to maintain.

Life is about having something that fulfills a purpose and

Escape the bonds.

The minimalist movement is seeking to instruct

people should focus their attention on things that are more

important things and distract you from them.

to the side. Being a part of the essential aside. Living with the indispensable

is better for you and for the entire world. It could improve your life and bring your happiness when you understand how to make the right investment

Your time and your energy and. Through incorporating

If you are minimalist, you can live the life you want with

greater focus. When you cut down on the things that distract you, you will have a better focus.

You can let distractions distract you, or find a better goal

more effectively. Take action now and

You will be able to fulfill your request. Reduce the amount

of the items that are vital, you profit

from a simpler way of life. And what do they mean?

What does that having a more simple life an

experiences where tasks and activities are

Optimized. You can use your time to other activities.

Things, money earns more and is used to

What is enough.

If you're looking to travel, or to spend time

with the people you cherish with the people you love, a simple existence

allows you. If you're planning to have fun, then life

and

Create

Good

memories

and

Experiences, living an easy life can help

it is your responsibility to complete homework and you must clean in

less time to devote to creating unforgettab

le moments.

Living a simple lifestyle isn't a way to live for the weak.

those who do not would like to be employed, however those

Know that the most important aspect goes far beyond the

materials and belongings, and the belongings and

need to be inside the house to be successful; accept yourself and know your

You. Simply put, the word minimalism entails that

Nothing external influences our inner peace.

I am confident that this is the correct route

It is definitely the best to me as well as my family.

There are different ways Yes, there are other ways. However, if you're looking for

in order to provide the chance to this kind of lifestyle, it's

It's worth a try.

Chapter 16: De-Cluttering And Organising Your Personal Items

The first step toward minimalism is organizing and clearing your personal belongings, including clothing and accessories books, music and electronic gadgets.

A house that is cluttered is a pain in the eye and can cause stress. It is possible that you are wondering, "how does de-cluttering lead to the idea of minimalism?" The answer is simple: de-cluttering does not just involve just about getting things organized and sorting it; it's also about getting rid items that don't serve any significance, purpose or worth.

If you choose to live a minimalist lifestyle by decluttering your personal possessions, but not doing similar to your habits and mental process, the process of de-cluttering can become a cycle. Soon after declutteringyour home, it will remain cluttered. Minimalism will help you stay out of the vicious cycle of decluttering.

To organize and de-clutter your life take these steps:

Step 1: Design an agenda

If you make a plan it's much easy to get started and stay determined to finish any task. A schedule can help you organize your belongings and keep them in a systematic and time-bound method. To create a decluttering plan take these steps:

Decide the amount of time you'll dedicate to de-cluttering and organizing your personal possessions. For example, based on your lifestyle and personal possessions, you might require an hour to sort your electronics, half a day to arrange your books, one day to sort your music and three days to sort your clothing and other accessories.

Start with one kind of item, and don't change to a different type until you've completely cleared and arrange that specific sort of item.

Set reasonable goals and do not go overboard. If you are a bit overwhelmed by items and clothes Do not take three days decluttering or reducing them. Instead, work through it in small steps and allow an entire week to get completed.

Step 2: Decide what you value the most

In order to begin cleaning out your personal possessions, you must begin at the beginning. To determine where you should begin, determine the things you value the most. Here's a great method of determining what you most value:

1. A Fire-Clause: Consider what you'd take in the event that there was the possibility of a fire. For example, the answer might be your wedding or family photo album, your phone laptop, computer, and chargers. The answer to this question will make you think and let you know that you don't need many things to be able to survive.

2. A Function Clause can help to determine the function of your belongings. If on the table beside you is a lamp that you have not used for 2 years, you should get rid of it as it's not serving its purpose. it's just occupying space.

3. The Someday Clause The Someday Clause have things that you think you'll use "someday" and we all do. Eliminate these things because that day won't come,

or when it does, you'll not be able to enjoy that item.

Perhaps, for instance, you have owned a piece of clothing that you did not wear, but kept it for "someday". However, it transpired that by the time'someday was finally here, the item was no longer fashionable any more.

4. A Happiness Clause All of us have possessions that are sentimental; the happiness clause is a way to point at them. If something you own does not serve a purpose, but holds it has a significant meaning then keep it.

For instance, you might decide to keep an infant's romper following birth. But, AVOID applying the happiness clause to each object by claiming that you like the item and can't let it go. Only a handful of objects fall in this category.

Step 3: Go on with the job

Once you've established a timetable and an idea of what is important to you begin to implement it.

1. Make sure you clear the area: First clean the area you're planning to arrange.

Closet: Pull out all your clothes and put them aside. Utilize a semi-wet, damp cloth to wash your closet, and allow it to dry.

Accessory: If you keep the accessories you have in one place, get them out and scrub the drawer. If you have boxes for different items like jewelry, watches caps, etc. similar, empty each box and scrub it.

Gadgets: In the event of gadgets, wash each (the exterior part) using a dry , clean cloth and then organize it by deleting any unnecessary photographs, files and folders.

Music: Take out your records and CDs rack or shelf and scrub it.

Books: Take the books on their shelves with a dry cloth or a vacuum and dust each book and stack them up. Make use of a semi-wetted piece of cloth to wipe the shelves and allow it to dry.

2. Start Discarding: For every type of personal item you should have a container labeled "discard". With distinct boxes to store each possession begin to throw away things you don't need Use the process described in the second step above to figure out what is most important to you.

Get rid of CDs you don't listen to, toss clothes that you do not wear, dispose of any gadgets by donating them away, or even selling them. You can also dispose of any unwanted accessories such as rings that you don't wear, watches that look similar and similar watches.

It is an crucial step since, as minimalists person, you don't require millions of things to be content You only need some. Don't let the burden of things you don't need make you feel guilty. Keep in mind the overall goal and purpose.

3. Organise and Restock: Last but not least organize, re-stock and arrange your personal possessions.

Closet: Check out what's left of your closet after throwing away clothes that are no longer needed and then begin to put it into your wardrobe. Hang the clothes you use frequently and fold them neatly and arrange your closet shelves. You can arrange your clothing according to color, use occasions, weather, and occasion. For example, you could hang your dresses for parties on one side, workwear in the middle, and casual clothes in another corner.

Accessories: To arrange your jewelry storage, make distinct boxes for accessories like bracelets and rings. You can also have one large container in which you can put those smaller boxes. Set similar items in the same place.

Gadgets: Put your most used gadgets on your table or create a drawer to store the gadgets.

The music industry has a variety of ways to arrange your music. You can arrange your music according to type and artist, or alphabetical order as well as release date. Based on your understanding in music theory, the most fascinating method of organizing your music is to organize it by artist. It is possible to do this by placing albums by the same artist.

Book: It is possible to arrange your books according to type, alphabetical sequence, and by author. Your shelf can be divided into various sections for your books, such as non-fiction, fiction, or horror comedy, thriller and even biography.

If you've followed these steps to eliminate clutter and arrange your belongings and personal items You will be able to reduce time and allow you to feel a sense of calm and happiness.

Conclusion

The book, with chance, will help you in deciding how you can live a minimalist lifestyle, and also help educate you about the ideal lifestyle. With your head cleared focus and commitment, you could start bringing back the pleasures of your life expand a bit, and cut down on other aspects of your lives that will make you more relaxed and happier. The journey towards becoming a minimalist require months of dedication hard work, hard painting, and a lot of creativity. If you stick to the plan and commit your time and energy to this new way of life you could reap the benefits for the rest of your life. Here are some key actions that I'll need to reiterate in your quest to be being a minimalist

Change your transportation habits

If you are able to rethink your travel habits it is possible to shop for in cash and get healthier in the process. Even though commuting on a motorbike may be not the ideal choice If you look at your daily schedule, you might find a trip towards the banking establishment or the supermarket that could be improved by a bicycle journey instead of drive.

Avoid Shopping

The best way to stay clear of buying unnecessary items is to avoid buying things you don't need. Be sure to only shop when you truly want something. Shopping trips on impulse usually end with the purchase of useless items.

Change Your Mindset Change Your Mindset, Change Your Lifestyle

If you are able to shift your perspective You can change the way you think about your lifestyle. If you come across a brand new item, think about what value it brings to your daily life. You'll begin to notice the increase in value over money. This is the first step towards living a more satisfying life.

Be grateful for what you Are able to

There are two kinds of people: people who wish and those who are thankful. The ones who would like to never find peace in their lives while they pursue their dreams. The ones who are content do not have anything they desire.

Beware of the Mainstream

Follow your own rhythm and stay clear of the popular. If you can recognize the major brands and trends and keep them in your closet You will not just shop there, but you could stand out from the crowd.

www.ingramcontent.com/pod-product-compliance
Lightning Source LLC
Chambersburg PA
CBHW071844080526
44589CB00012B/1102